MORE NETWORKING IDEAS continued

ASK QUESTIONS TO BEGIN CONVERSATIONS

- Use media headlines as conversation starters.
- Ask about other people's business products, services and goals.
- Find common interests in the community, business, hobbies, and families.
- Practice talking to strangers to enhance your skills. Good places to rehearse include elevators and lines at the supermarket, movie theater, bank and post office.

NETWORKING ETIQUETTE

- Don't monopolize anyone's time.
- Networking is more than belonging to and attending professional meetings. It is becoming involved in committees and activities, getting to know the needs of the organization and the membership.
- Networking requires you to share your relationships and resources with others.
- Networking requires constantly strengthening and activating the relationships that already exist and finding new ones to further develop and nurture.

SUCCESSFUL NETWORKERS

- Make others feel good about themselves.
- Use leadership skills to include others.
- Provide resources.
- Initiate opportunities for others.
- Are in the habit of introducing themselves by name to others.
- Introduce people they meet to others they know.
- Follow up immediately on new persons they have met.
- Never ask for a job or a contact at a social event.
- Don't put people on the spot by asking for something in front of others.
- Don't promise something they can't deliver.
- Maintain comfortable eye contact with the person to whom they are speaking.
- Don't look over their shoulder to see who else is there they want to meet.
- When they need to move on, don't leave a person standing alone. They include them by asking them to join you to meet another person.
- Excuse themselves when leaving one group to join another.
- Ask for business cards of others before they give out theirs.
- Avoid ethnic or gender jokes, gossip, rumors, and sarcasm.

THE ART OF CONVERSATION

CONVERSATION STARTERS:

Many people find it difficult to talk to people they don't know. The secret is that even if it is difficult, one can learn to engage others in meaningful, sincere conversation. They can also learn the difference between meaningless banter that drives everyone away and meaningful "small" talk. The key involves planning ahead.

"Have you been a member of the organization long?"
"Do you know today's speaker?"
"What do you like best about the group we are with?"
"Are you involved in any committees?"
"Is this city your home town?"

- Read newspapers and magazines for ideas about current events, but stay away from controversial issues unless you know the stance of others. You can ask for views about headline items, but never challenge them if your ideas are different.
- Sports news is always safe. If you are not a sports buff, it may be time to take up some new interests for conversations sake.

THE ART OF CONVERSATION continued

- Business ideas from the gurus are always welcome. Credit your sources. You will impress others with your ability to share information. Don't get too wordy or technical.
- Research other persons' businesses and industries to get some clues on their interests or accomplishments.
- Ask questions about their business, their products, their needs, and suggest people you know who may be helpful to them.
- Be a good listener.
- Don't butt into other's conversations. Join the group quietly and listen before speaking. If it appears to be a private conversation, excuse yourself and either walk away to join another group or ask if it is a private conversation. Courtesy always works.
- Remember the people to whom you are introducing yourself.
- Repeat the name of persons to whom you are being introduced. e.g. *"Mr. Cyrus, it is a pleasure to meet you."* At the same time, look for something about the person that is distinguishable and will help to recall their name when you meet again.
- Blend introductions with a warm smile and a firm handshake. Special reminder to women: learn how to use your entire hand, not just the fingertips, for a business-like greeting.

INTERESTING INTRODUCTIONS FOR LARGE GROUP GATHERINGS

Have a 7-second introduction ready for different occasions. Prepare it so that follow-up questions can be asked. Use your name at the end of the introduction. To do so promotes you and your business and helps others to remember you after the gathering is over. Some examples:

- *"Good morning, my real estate business takes me into the homes of the rich and famous. I hope you will add your name to my list. My name is Jake Sydney of Sunbelt Real Estate."*
- *"Hello, I am a matchmaker for Berke Durant and Associates, an executive recruiting organization. Call me when you are looking for the best employees. I am Matthew Hunter."*
- *"If you love the night scene, going out for dinner, the movies, dancing and partying without having to worry about the security of your home while you're out, ATC Security Systems is the company to call. I am Allan Todd."*

NAMETAGS

Most large events have nametags on which you write your name and company affiliation.

- If space is limited, consider writing your first name in large print with your company name.
- Always attach it to your right lapel. It is where the eye naturally goes when shaking hands.
- To increase your professional image, have a name badge professionally prepared to include your full name and company name. Wear it only at business functions.

BUSINESS CARDS - YOURS AND OTHERS'

Treat business cards as you would an invitation to a very important event. They can, if properly used, be an entrée to new business relationships, new friends, new information, and new opportunities. They should be a reflection of the image you want to portray.

- Quality printing on good card stock in business colors should be considered to increase your credibility. The adage, "to be successful, you must look successful" applies to business cards e.g., don't use pink or light blue if you are a financial planner.

BUSINESS CARDS - YOURS AND OTHERS' continued

- Unless you have a distinctive logo that has been designed for you, omit standard ones that others also use.
- Keep information on cards simple and easy to read. They may be scanned into someone's computer Rolodex and too much information may confuse the technology. The important things like your name, company name, telephone numbers, e-mail address and fax number should stand out.
- If you use a new technology like a CD-ROM for your card, make certain your network has the technology to access the information.
- If you are not working, have cards printed with pertinent information which allows others to reach you. Name, telephone, fax, and e-mail address will do. If you want, you may put your home address on the card. Consider renting a PO Box.
- Never use a business card with incorrect information that has been crossed out. Either print new ones inexpensively on your own computer, or find a printer who has reasonable prices. Your business card is a reflection of you and how you operate professionally.
- At meetings and other events, keep your cards in a jacket, skirt or pants pocket so that they are readily accessible. Fumbling for cards in inaccessible pockets or handbags can be annoying to others.
- After you have left the meeting or event use the backs of cards to jot down ***where*** you met the person, ***when*** and ***how*** you need to follow up.
- Keep an extra supply of cards in your car trunk so that you don't run out or attend a meeting or event unprepared.
- When you collect others' cards, remember they are to be used only for appropriate follow-ups. Don't give someone else's card to a third party without permission.
- Make certain your cards can be easily read. Select a type font that is large and clear enough so that even Baby Boomers (who are now turning the forty plus mark) do not have to read them at arms length.
- Devise a system for the cards you have collected. If you do not have a computer, clip cards together by event, date, business or some other way that is meaningful to you. Filing a card is helpful only if you can retrieve it by remembering the name and the reason you wanted to contact that person.

COMMUNICATION

E-MAIL

E-mail is an easy way to keep in touch with your network, but don't abuse it.

- Keep messages brief.
- Avoid sending jokes and other forwarded information from others.
- Spell check and edit messages.
- Avoid personal messages on business e-mail.
- Be politically correct.

TELEPHONE/VOICEMAIL

- Keep messages very brief and professional.
- Repeat your phone number twice slowly.
- Suggest times when you can be reached easily to avoid that old telephone tag game.
- When calling persons you have met at a networking meeting, have a script ready so that you can be brief and to the point. Re-introduce yourself to refresh their memory.
- If persons you are calling can't meet with you or give you the information you need, be gracious, and thank them for their time. Ask if it is o.k. for you to stay in contact. Don't oversell or put them on the spot.
- If your calls don't get answered after three attempts, a brief note may be sent as a follow-up. Don't be frustrated when people don't get back to you as quickly as you would like. They may be very busy and your needs are not a priority to them. Follow-up with an appropriate message recognizing how busy they are, and ask for a better contact time or person.

COMMUNICATION continued

WRITTEN COMMUNICATIONS

Brief notes, cleverly written cards and post cards are appropriate and always appreciated. They may be used for:

- Congratulatory messages for special events, promotions, new contracts, etc.
- To accompany published information of interest that someone may have missed.
- To say thank you for a referral or lead.
- To remember special occasions and holidays.

When printing and mailing cards:

- Avoid mailing labels; they are for mass mailings, not personalized notes.
- Use heavy stock notepaper. Go first class.
- Some experts advise using commemorative stamps instead of postage meters for that personal touch.

NETWORKING AND REFERRAL GROUPS

They are becoming more and more popular.

- Usually consists of one representative from each business and industry.
- Each person is required to provide referrals to other members.
- Meets weekly or monthly.
- Can be found through Chambers of Commerce, newspaper listings or from other business contacts.
- Usually includes a fee for joining and requires minimum attendance.
- Gives you opportunity for positioning yourself as an expert.
- If the group does not provide leads within several months, seek out others or form one of your own.

CAREER SEARCH NETWORKING

Networking accounts for more than 60% of all new jobs. The higher the level of the position, the more this is true. Think of all the job resources as a large pie.

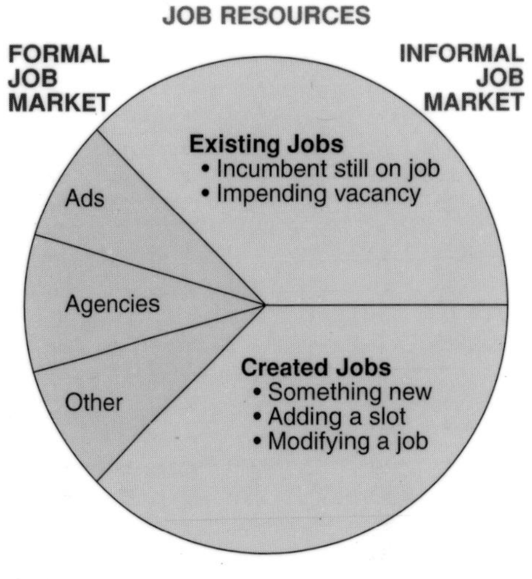
JOB RESOURCES
FORMAL JOB MARKET
INFORMAL JOB MARKET
Existing Jobs
• Incumbent still on job
• Impending vacancy
Ads
Agencies
Other
Created Jobs
• Something new
• Adding a slot
• Modifying a job

- The **formal job market** consists of your strongest job competition. 80% of the people looking for a job use these resources, which are only 20% of the market. This market includes all positions that a company or organization has publicized through such methods as an ad, an employment agency or a search firm. As soon as a position is openly communicated in the formal market, the selection process becomes competitive.
- The **informal market** consists of the best job opportunities. Of the people looking for jobs, 20% use this method, which accounts for 80% of possibilities. This market includes all positions - in varying stages that have not yet been communicated through formal market channels (including self-employment).

CAREER SEARCH NETWORKING continued

In order to gain access to the informal market, you must locate and approach the appropriate decision-makers. If you can identify a need within an organization before it is publicized as a job description in the formal market, you will significantly reduce, if not eliminate, the competition.

SEARCH STRATEGIES

- It is estimated that somewhere between 75 to 85% of actual job openings are not listed in newspapers or other public listings.
- These jobs, often referred to as **the hidden job market**, are usually filled by people who are acquainted with current company employees, or by a person who has made the company aware of their qualifications through some form of direct contact. Therefore, **networking** and **direct contact** will be vital components of an effective job search. There are four basic job search methods:

Networking

- This involves contacting colleagues, coworkers, friends, relatives, former supervisors, neighbors and other acquaintances in order to enlist their aid in your job search. According to Department of Labor statistics, most people employed are hired via this method.

Direct Contact

- This method targets companies that employ people with your skills and experience. Without waiting for a listing, contact the company by a visit, phone call or resume and cover letter. According to Department of Labor statistics, 24 % of people employed are hired via this method.

Use of Employment Services

- In this method you contact one or several agencies to aid in your job search. According to Department of Labor statistics, 6% of people employed are hired via this method.

Classified Ads

- This method requires you call or send resumes for listings that are in newspapers. According to statistics, 5% of people employed are hired via classified ads.

This is not an exhaustive list of job search methods, but these four will form the basis of your action plan for networking as an effective job search tool.

BUILDING A NETWORK

...takes time and careful record keeping.

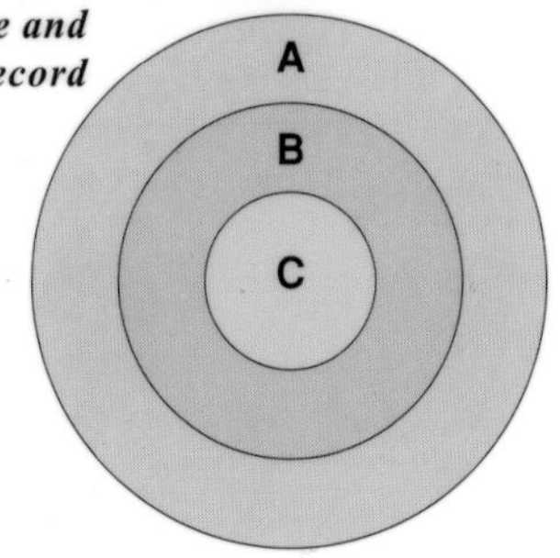
A
B
C

A - Contacts
- Already known to you
- Instant rapport
- Feedback on your presentation
- Referrals to B - Contacts

B - Contacts
- Bridge people
- Information resources on:
  - Activities, people and events in the field
  - Needs and problems in the field
  - Further refinement of objective focus
- Referrals to other B and to C - Contacts

C - Contacts
- Can make decisions
- Can receive proposals
- Can create jobs
- Referrals to other C - Contacts

- Networking is making the initial contact a lasting and beneficial one to everyone involved.
- Never appear weak, needy, or too pushy and aggressive.
- Networking agendas need not be impersonal and manipulative.
- One must be well organized and persistent to create an effective network.
- Networking is time consuming and a great deal of hard work, but can add fun and variety to your life.
- Networking can put you in touch with people you admire, but you must make the first call.
- Networking fulfills a basic human need for relationships and interaction with others. It does not mean you have to always function in large groups. It can give you quality time with a few people or business acquaintances at a time.
- Do not make idle promises; always be sincere, and avoid inconsiderate, inappropriate, unprofessional or shortsighted behaviors that can produce a negative impact on the people. Always work toward developing and maintaining purposeful relationships.

QUESTIONS TO ASK YOURSELF AND OTHER CLOSE ASSOCIATES COULD INCLUDE:

- Have I ever been rude to that person or to others in their presence?
- Have I been too focused on sales?
- Do I interrupt others?
- Do I exaggerate my knowledge or sphere of influence?
- Am I guilty of not paying attention to people who are speaking to me?
- Do I monopolize conversations?
- Do I include others when asking for and receiving what I want or need?
- Do I make it clear that when I give information, leads, referrals, etc., there are no strings attached?
- Do I project a professional image in dress, speech, and mannerisms?

If people are avoiding you, don't blame them; evaluate your actions first AND/OR ask a personal or professional coach for help.

A NETWORKING QUIZ

____Do you know what values are important to you?
____Do you have a written list of goals and action strategies to reach them?
____Do you know who is in your network?
____Do you have an interesting introduction?
____Do you present a professional image?
____Do you engage other people in conversation?
____Do you introduce others to people you know?
____Do you keep your business cards ready at events?
____Do you follow up on leads and referrals quickly?
____Do you focus on quality rather than quantity of leads and referrals, allowing them to be managed in an appropriate and timely manner?
____Do you belong to and participate in professional, trade, and civic/charitable organizations?
____Do you have a system for organizing business cards for further contacts?
____Do you follow-up with your networking contacts frequently and effectively?
____Do you have a clear purpose for attending events and meetings?
____Do you participate in meetings and activities?
____Do you offer your assistance to others?
____Are you courteous when you meet new people?
____Do you read professional and trade journals related to your industry and the industries of your network?
____Do you read articles and books that will increase and reinforce your networking skills?

A "no" answer to any of these questions indicates where you need to focus on developing more effective networking skills.

NETWORKING LETTER FOR JOB SEARCH

This letter asks for information only, and includes the important referral resource, an action step, and requests for other networking contacts.

October 23, 2000

Mr. Dave Berke
222 Military Road
Boca Raton, Florida 20910

Dear Mr. Berke,

INTRODUCTION

Joanne Ashley of BarCharts, Inc. suggested that I contact you about your leadership role in the human resources industry. As the CEO of BDA Lincolnshire International, you are in a position to give me some much needed advice about career opportunities in the Southeast. Your insights would be very valuable for a person with my experience who is contemplating a move into the area.

BACKGROUND INFORMATION

After receiving an MBA with a concentration in Human Resources from Michigan State University, I worked for three years for Berger Electronics. My responsibilities included special projects related to recruiting, organizational development and succession planning.

REASON FOR WRITING

I am certain that you are aware that recent mergers, acquisitions, and company reorganizations have affected many people in my industry. As a result of such a merger, I am challenged to search for a new career opportunity. After careful thought and research, it is clear to me that I would like to continue my career in Human Resources in a growing business environment in South Florida where I will be able to contribute in a meaningful way.

ACTION STEP

I would like to discuss with you how my background fits into the South Florida market, and, if you have any advice or resources that might assist me in my career search. I will call your office to set up a convenient time for us to meet when I am in the area at the end of next month. At that time, I am hoping that you will also be able to give me the names of other persons with whom I should try to meet. I realize that you are a very busy person with multiple business priorities, but I appreciate any time that you are able to spare.

Sincerely,

Marilyn Alexander

NETWORKING LETTER AFTER MEETING SOMEONE AT A LARGE GATHERING

This follow-up letter compliments the person, reminds them when the meeting took place, lets the person know you did business with their referrals, and gave them credit for the arrangement. It also has a further action step.

October 23, 2000

Mr. J. B. Glaser
CEG Corporation
401 City Place
W. Palm Beach, Florida 76543

Dear Mr. Glaser,

INTRODUCTION AND APPRECIATION

Your presentation at the Chamber of Commerce last week was excellent. The information was timely and pertinent to many areas of my business and I wanted to thank you for taking the time to share it with the membership.

FOLLOW UP - NETWORK REFERALS

I have made appointments with several of the persons to whom you referred and they also, were helpful. When I mentioned your name, they asked me to convey their best wishes to you. It was obvious to me that you are indeed held in high asteem.

FURTHER ACTION STEP

After doing some research, I have an idea that I would like to share with you that could possibly benefit your expansion plans. If you are free for lunch a week from next Thursday, I would like you to be my guest. I will call your office at the end of this week to confirm.

Cordially,

Clare Landen

PRICE: U.S. $4.95 CAN $7.50

ISBN 157222488-6

50495

March 2001

SOME HELPFUL NETWORKING TIPS

NETWORKING EXPANSION THROUGH VOLUNTEERISM AND SPECIAL INTEREST GROUPS

Increasing your network does not have to happen only through business events and trade organizations.

- Serving on boards of non-profit organizations and in leadership positions for charitable fundraisers will increase networking power. You meet new people and establish trustworthy relationships that go beyond self-service. The returns on this type of networking can be dramatic.
- Professional development seminars and courses of study add to your knowledge base and increase opportunities for building ties with new people with common interests.
- Special interests involving hobbies, sporting and cultural events are bonus activities for networkers. They allow you to balance your lifestyle and can increase family involvement.

IF YOU NEED HELP REMEMBERING NAMES OR FACES

Some people never remember names or faces. This is a real deficit to effective networking. The brain is a biological and electrical switchboard that makes sense of our activities. The more we use it, the better trained it becomes. Focus on the person you are meeting. Repeat their name and use associations to develop a better memory system. Memory systems rely on:

- Observation
- Concentration
- Visualization
- Association
- Substitution
- Classification
- Linking

Practice memory skills and read the memory enhancing books that are available.

USE THE INTERNET

The internet is a valuable tool and provides multiple resources for active networking.

- Research information about products and services to know more about your existing contacts and to provide timely information to potential contacts. Using this information increases your credibility and resources.
- Create a Web page to market your products and services. Refer new contacts to it. In this age of information technology, well-done Web pages are necessary for most businesses. Make certain it is updated on a regular basis. Follow up immediately on inquiries.

Other Business related reference guides available:
- **Business Ethics**
- **Business Letters**
- **Business Research**
- **Resumes and Interviews**
- **Personal Finance**
- **Managerial Skills**
- **How to start a Home Based Business**

INTRODUCTION

To build a solid foundation for networking, create a list of persons with whom you meet regularly. Assess your influence with these people, how often you have given them information and referrals, and how often you receive referrals, contacts or useful business information. If you find that you are giving more than receiving, you might want to call your closest contacts to discuss your concern about your lack of networking success. Ask for their advice or assistance.

Networking can create new business and career opportunities if people assess, evaluate, and prioritize their approach to potential customers, clients and employers.

- *Effective networking is NOT **selling, using people strictly for gain, manipulating others, putting friends, neighbors, or associates on the spot, or badgering people about business or potential job openings.** Networking IS an **attitude involving** building relationships and resources. It requires you to share your relationships and resources with others.*

ALSO
- It is not a quick fix or a magic potion for meeting new people.
- It is more than belonging to and attending professional meetings. It is becoming involved in committees and activities, getting to know the needs of the organization and the membership.
- Networking involves constantly strengthening and activating the relationships that already exist and finding new ones to further develop and nurture. You get back what you put into it.

DID YOU KNOW ?

- Referrals generate 80% more results than cold calls.
- Approximately 60% of all new contracts and/or jobs are found through networking - most people we meet have at least 250 contacts. Therefore, if effective marketing techniques are used, a new contract, new business venture, or a new job is only two to three people away.
- Effective networking is a learned skill. Anyone who wants to learn can become an effective network agent.
- Networking requires constant improvement of approaches to those already in the network, while at the same time, building new contacts.
- Networking is NOT just exchanging business cards and knowing a lot of people. It is creating follow-up strategies for the people whose business cards you have.
- Advances in technology and the shifting interests and needs of a global economic society contribute to the increased popularity and usefulness of networking.
- Fact: It is predicted that the focus on networking will continue to grow. The success of every business and every person will greatly depend on making their "nets" work.

DEFINITIONS AND ORIGINS OF THE TERM "NETWORKS"

- A series of interconnected wires and cables formed to bring information, news, scandals, gossip, and other relevant information to the public.
- A process to gather and disseminate information effectively to produce results.
- A blueprint for sharing leads, ideas, and expertise with one another.
- A direction for accomplishing goals through the power of synergy and teamwork.
- A mode to verify the accuracy and validity of information and ideas.
- A formula to promote a product, service, or idea.

EFFECTIVE NETWORKING:

- Increases productivity by using resources and opportunities wisely.
- Creates greater results in less time by maximizing interactions and conversations.
- Replaces the weak areas of one person with the strength of a group or a team.
- Reduces the power of your competition and keeps you abreast with your competition.
- Provides new experiences anywhere in the world. Everyone has contacts who know people who know people.
- Makes you look good, supports your efforts and expands your financial and professional reach.

HOW TO NETWORK AT EVENTS AND MEETINGS

OFTEN CALLED "WORKING THE ROOM"

Before you attend an event, ask yourself what you want to accomplish both on a professional level and on a personal level. Develop an action plan with expected results. Know who will be attending these meetings. Are they a part of your industry? Will the program enhance your professional knowledge or development?

- How can you take part or be visible in the program?
- Identify benefits before the event. What are the compensations and the rewards?
- How can you establish new ways to communicate, make connections, and establish rapport with others attending the event?
- Where are the opportunities to increase your resource base, potential clients or employers?
- How and where can you gain insight; learn new information and knowledge?
- Will this event produce increased business and income?
- How can this event enhance my career opportunities?
- Will I have fun?

GUIDELINES FOR WORKING A ROOM

Getting Past Old Messages/Tapes- Strangers are no longer "bad" people we were warned to stay away from when we were children.

- You're really not with strangers...you have a common interest, e.g., chamber meetings, a new charitable or political organization, and the health club. As you approach a "stranger" at a meeting or event, remember the purpose of the event and determine commonalities that might be present. Develop conversation starters for these events to get the conversation going.
  - In the past, proper etiquette has taught us to wait to be properly introduced.
  - We must learn to introduce ourselves. Develop and practice self-introduction that is clear, interesting and well delivered. Make certain your introduction is energetic... have different intros for business and social events.
- "Good things come to those who wait"
  - Waiting for people to find you and introduce themselves won't happen because it's just as difficult for them as it for you. Leaders and successful people have learned to overcome their shyness. They don't wait. They reach out and extend themselves. Shyness is a learned response which can be eliminated with training and practice and your communication skills.
- Use your host behavior as a networking strategy.
  - Hosts greet others, begin conversations, introduce people to one another and make certain they are comfortable. At professional functions, volunteer to be on the greeting or sign-in committee.
  - Develop a retrieval and time system to keep in touch with persons in your "Rolodex" files. Don't let them forget you because you have not developed an appropriate follow-up system.
- Avoid talking exclusively to and sitting with persons you already know at meetings and large events.

YOU ARE THE CENTER OF YOUR NETWORK

- Start a network diagram from your Rolodex. A network diagram provides a visual representation of the diversity and magnitude of your network. To draw your diagram, take a single sheet of paper and write your name in the middle of the page as the hub of your network. From this hub, draw lines representing the major spokes of your network, i.e., family, business associates, clubs, church members, alumni groups, etc. Each spoke should have branches for the key individuals in each of the major areas. The diagram will provide a new organization and a greater awareness of the resources you have available.

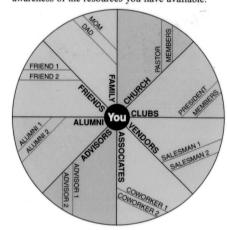

Whenever you start a new project or are looking for the right people for support or advice, your diagram will help you identify, plan, and implement your networking approach. When you want to contact a certain individual, look at your diagram to see who can be the link to help you make that contact.

LIST MAJOR ACHIEVEMENTS IN YOUR LIFE:

- Gives insight into what you can share with others. You are the only one who really knows the significance of each accomplishment in your life - whether they seem small or large, significant, easy or difficult - be proud of them. Keep accomplishments clear and in the forefront of your thinking. It will help you share the benefits and expertise with others.

COMPLETE THE FOLLOWING:

I am...
Good at:
Experienced with:
The source of:
Trained in:
Keep adding to this list to increase your professional competence.

MORE NETWORKING IDEAS

- Give up the "Doing It All by Myself" mentality.
- Develop a "Power Presentation" to enhance the way you are perceived. A "Powerful" perception is one where you appear to be someone others find credible, likeable, knowledgeable, and caring...
- There is no Number One. Everyone is important.
- Give first, you will receive back.
- Learn the art of conversation.
- Meet new people.